HEINEMANN Profiles

Mother Teresa

An Unauthorized Biography

Haydn Middleton

Heinemann Library
Chicago, Illinois

© 2001 Reed Educational & Professional Publishing
Published by Heinemann Library,
an imprint of Reed Educational & Professional Publishing,
100 N. LaSalle, Suite 1010
Chicago, IL 60602
Customer Service 888-454-2279
Visit our website at www.heinemannlibrary.com

Designed by Visual Image
Originated by Dot Gradations
Printed in Hong Kong

05 04 03 02 01
10 9 8 7 6 5 4 3 2 1

Library of Congress Cataloging-in-Publication Data
Middleton, Haydn.
  Mother Teresa / Haydn Middleton.
    p. cm. – (Heinemann profiles)
  Includes bibliographical references and index.
  Summary: A biography of the nun who founded the Missionaries of Charity, gained wide recognition for her work with the destitute and dying in Calcutta and elsewhere, and was awarded the Nobel Piece Prize in 1979.
    ISBN 1-57572-227-5 (library binding)
    1. Teresa, Mother, 1910---Juvenile literature. 2. Missionaries of Charity—Biography—Juvenile literature. 3. Nuns—India—Calcutta—Biography—Juvenile literature. [1. Teresa, Mother, 1910- 2. Missionaries of Charity. 3. Missionaries. 4. Nuns. 5. Women—Biography. 6. Nobel Prizes—Biography.] I. Title. II. Series.

BX4406.5.Z8 M53 2000
271'.97—dc21
[B]   99-089881

Acknowledgments
The Publishers would like to thank the following for permission to reproduce photographs: AKG Photo, p. 6; Associated Press, pp. 4, 5, 12, 20, 35, 45, 47, 51, 53; BBC, p. 32; Corbis/Hulton-Deutsch, p. 22; Rex Features, pp. 25, 28, 33, 36, 40, 42, Rex Features/Jobard, p. 49; Rex Features/D. Ludwig, p. 46; Rex Features/J. Rogers, p. 43; Sipa Press/R. Trippett, p. 37; Trip/J. Randall, p. 14; Trip/H. Rogers, pp. 26, 31; Trip/B. Turner, p. 39.

Cover photograph reproduced with permission of Rex Features.

Every effort has been made to contact copyright holders of any material reproduced in this book. Any omissions will be rectified in subsequent printings if notice is given to the Publisher.

Some words are shown in bold, **like this.** You can find out what they mean by looking in the glossary.

This is an unauthorized biography. The subject has not sponsored or endorsed this book.

CONTENTS

WHO WAS MOTHER TERESA?

Mother Teresa of Calcutta, the "Saint of the Slums," never claimed to be anyone special. When people wanted to write her biography, she could not understand why. "I am just a little pencil in God's hand," she would say. She devoted most of her life to helping the poorest of the poor, first in India, and afterwards in many other countries. Until the 1960s, she was not well-known outside India. Then the **media** made her world famous, and she won many prizes and awards for her work. In 1979, she was awarded the **prestigious** Nobel Peace Prize, which she received with her usual **humility**.

Even in old age, Mother Teresa continued her work.

SAINT OR SINNER?

For years, Mother Teresa was seen as a living, breathing saint. British journalist Christopher Hitchens once called her "the least criticized human being on earth." That all changed towards the end of her life. In the late twentieth century, the world was a very different place from the one in which Mother Teresa had begun her work. In the 1990s, some people accused her of not keeping up with the times. On issues

An opponent of abortion, Mother Teresa believed that "there can never be enough" children.

such as abortion, technology, women's rights, and poverty relief, they called her views old-fashioned and even cruel. At her death in 1997, she was saluted as one of the world's great **humanitarians,** but the debate continues about the true impact and value of her work.

"Mother Teresa inspired many people with whom she came into contact not because she preached powerful sermons but because she demonstrated a way, not always effective, of using the power of love as a force for healing and **redemption.** In spite of all the criticism leveled against her, Mother Teresa gave tens of thousands of people the opportunity to express their love for their fellow human beings." From *Mother Teresa: Beyond the Image* by Anne Sebba, 1997

BALKAN BEGINNINGS

Mother Teresa won fame for her work in Calcutta, one of India's largest cities. She became an Indian citizen in 1949, but she was not an Indian by birth, nor was her real name Teresa. That was the name she took when she became a nun. She was born on August 26, 1910, in a war-torn southeastern part of Europe known as the **Balkans.** Her Roman Catholic parents, Nikola and Drana Bojaxhiu, had two other children: Age, a girl, and Lazar, a boy. On the day after the new baby was born, she was **baptized** Agnes Gonxha.

The marketplace was the center of the town of Skopje early in the twentieth century.

"Mine was a happy family," Mother Teresa said in later life. "I had one brother and one sister, but I do not like to talk about it. It is not important now. The important thing is to follow God's way, the way he leads us to do something beautiful for him." It is not easy to discover details about the early life of Agnes Gonxha. Her hometown of Skopje is now part of Macedonia. When Agnes was born, it was a part of the Ottoman Empire, ruled by the Turks.

LIVING CLOSE TO DEATH

The Bojaxhiu family was neither Macedonian nor Turkish, but Albanian. For hundreds of years, the Albanian people had no country of their own, and many of them, like Agnes' father, campaigned for an **independent** homeland. In 1912, after a war in the Balkans, a small Albania was created, but half of the Albanian population—including the Bojaxhiu family—still lived outside its borders.

GONXHA THE GIRL

Gonxha means "flower bud," and that was what Agnes's family usually called her. Many Albanians today still know her by this name. Although she was not the best student in her class, she enjoyed singing and was a good mandolin player. Her brother, Lazar, said she was sensible, serious, and deeply religious, even as a little girl. She would scold him whenever he helped himself to jam during the night, because they were not supposed to touch food after midnight if they were going to attend **Mass** and receive **Communion** with their mother in the morning.

CHANGING FAMILY FORTUNES

Agnes stands with her Skopje school friends at the age of ten.

Her father, Nikola, was a successful businessman, and his work often took him **abroad.** Agnes liked to hear his stories about his travels. Maybe it gave her an appetite to see the world for herself when she

was older. Nikola also pushed hard for a Greater Albania in which all Albanians could live together. His position was not popular with everyone, and he made many enemies in the **Balkans.** After a political dinner in 1918, he died suddenly—possibly from poisoning.

Times were hard for the Bojaxhiu family after Nikola's death. Agnes's mother, Drana, made ends meet by setting up her own embroidery and textile business. Although she was poor herself, she still helped those who were poorer. As a child, Agnes thought the regular guests at mealtimes were relatives. Later, she discovered that they were complete strangers. Her **devout** mother's kindness and **hospitality** made a great impression on the growing girl. She also took to heart this piece of her mother's advice: "When you do good, do it quietly, as if you were throwing a stone into the sea."

"I remember my mother, my father, and the rest of us praying together each evening… It is God's greatest gift to the family. It maintains family unity. The family that does not pray together does not stay together."
Mother Teresa

Agnes (seated) was close to Age and Lazar.

IN AND OUT OF CHURCH

The Roman Catholic Church of the Sacred Heart in Skopje played an important part in the life of the Bojaxhiu family. They worshiped there, and both Agnes and her sister, Age, sang in the church choir, even though Agnes had some health problems, including **chronic** coughs. According to Lazar, his mother and sisters spent so much time in the church that they seemed to live there as much as they did at home.

Agnes sits next to her sister, Age (with parasol), on a visit to Nerezima.

Every year, groups of Catholics and non-Catholics from the area would make a **pilgrimage** to the chapel of the Madonna of Letnice. Agnes's mother arranged for her to visit the **shrine** at other times, too—to pray alone in the chapel.

Joy…is a compass

Unlike many women who become nuns, Agnes had no sudden vision to convince her of what she had to do. When she asked Father Jambrekovic if God really was calling her, he answered that if she felt joy, then that might mean it was a true call. "Joy that comes from the depths of your being," he told her, "is like a compass by which you can tell what direction your life should follow."

HOW COULD SHE BE SURE?

Even at the age of twelve, Agnes took comfort and strength from prayer. Already she sensed that perhaps she would become a nun in later life and devote her life to God—perhaps through teaching—but she needed to be sure about taking such a big step.

As she grew older, she had many talks about her future with two important members of the church. One was Monsignor Janez Gnidovec. He was bishop of Skopje from 1924 to 1939, and was a close friend of the Bojaxhiu family. The other was Father Franjo Jambrekovic, who became **pastor** of Sacred Heart Church in 1925. He started a library and set up a Christian youth group called the **Sodality** of the Blessed Virgin Mary. Agnes was greatly inspired by her participation in the youth group, and began to show interest in the work of **missionaries** in India.

In October 1981, an Australian journalist asked whether the "mother of thousands" missed having a child of her own. "Naturally, naturally, of course," she replied. "That is the sacrifice we make. That is the gift we give to God."

"WHAT WILL I DO FOR CHRIST?"

Father Jambrekovic told the girls of the **sodality** about the **Jesuits.** The Jesuit **order** was founded in 1534 by Ignatius Loyola, a Spanish Catholic, who later became a saint. Its original goals were to protect Catholicism against the challenges of the **Protestant Reformation** and to carry out **missionary** work. Agnes was interested to learn from Father Jambrekovic that Jesuit missionaries from the **Balkans** had gone to Bengal, India, in 1924. She also thought hard about these questions in Loyola's book, *Spiritual Exercises:* "What have I done for Christ, what am I doing for Christ, and what will I do for Christ?" She began to feel quite sure that Christ was calling her to serve him as a missionary nun.

THE NEED FOR SELF-SACRIFICE

Deciding to be a nun is not really like choosing to be an artist or an athlete. Agnes believed that if she truly was being called, then she had no choice in the matter at all. God's will simply had to be done. That meant accepting that she would never marry or have her own family—two things nuns are not allowed to do. This would not be easy, because Agnes had always liked children. However, she finally told her mother that she would become a nun. Drana was not surprised by her daughter's decision, and supported her choice. "Put your hand in His," she told Agnes, "and walk all the way with Him."

Agnes also wrote with her news to her brother, Lazar, an army officer who was about to become an **equerry** to the new King Zog of Albania. He wrote back, asking a little sharply if she really knew what she was doing. "You think you are important because you are an officer serving a king with two million subjects," Agnes replied. "But I am serving the King of the whole world."

IRISH INTERLUDE

Agnes chose to join the Loreto Sisters. This group, based in Rathfarnham, Ireland, was a branch of one of the leading **orders** of nuns: the Institute of the Blessed Virgin Mary (IBVM).

Thérèse of Lisieux

There are two notable Saint Teresas in the Roman Catholic Church. The more famous is Teresa of Avila (1515–82), at right, an **aristocratic** Spanish nun whose spiritual writings are still read today. But Agnes named herself after the lesser-known Thérèse of Lisieux (1873–97), the daughter of a French watchmaker. Known as the "Little Flower," this saint, who died at the age of 24,  inspired others with her deep but simple faith in God. She believed that it was possible to serve God by doing the most ordinary little jobs cheerfully and well.

She knew that nuns from this **order** were often sent as **missionaries** to India. In September 1928, at the age of eighteen, she left home for Zagreb, where she was joined by Betika Kajnc, another young woman who wished to become a Loreto Sister.

They did not go directly to Loreto Abbey at Rathfarnham. First they traveled by train to Paris, where they were interviewed by Mother Eugene MacAvin. She was impressed with their seriousness, so she sent them on, with her recommendation, to Ireland.

A CHANGE OF NAME

At Loreto Abbey, Agnes began training to be a nun. Besides learning about the order's work, she also studied English. This would be useful when she moved to India, which in 1928 was still a part of the British Empire, with English as the official language. Now she was no longer called Agnes—she took the religious name of Sister Teresa, spelling it without an "h" to avoid confusion with another nun's name. In many ways, she was breaking away from her past.

This photo of Agnes (top) at her school graduation was taken in 1928, when she was eighteen, shortly before she left to join the Loreto Sisters in Ireland. Her mother and sister would never see her again.

INTO INDIA

In December 1928, Sister Teresa set off on the voyage that had been in her mind for so many years. It was a long trip: through the Suez Canal, the Red Sea, the Indian Ocean, and into the Bay of Bengal. The street scenes—and the poverty—that she found in India were a world away from Skopje.

"A GREAT GIRL, FULL OF FUN"

In Darjeeling, at the foot of the Himalayas, Teresa began her novitiate—the first steps a nun must make towards taking her final **vows.** She taught at the Loreto **convent** school there, and helped out at the

Sister Teresa (left) and this **novice** nun lived at Darjeeling in 1929. The heavy black **habits** must have been uncomfortable to wear in India's hot climate.

16

First impressions

Sister Teresa's first impressions of India were so strong that she had to write them down. Of the city of Madras, she wrote: "Many families live in the streets, along the city walls, even in places thronged with people. Day and night they live out in the open on mats they have made from large palm leaves—or frequently on the bare ground. They are all virtually naked, wearing at best a ragged loincloth… As we went along the street we chanced upon one family gathered around a dead relation, wrapped in worn red rags, strewn with yellow flowers, his face painted in colored stripes. It was a horrifying scene. If our people could only see all this, they would stop grumbling about their own misfortunes and offer thanks to God for blessing them with such abundance."

small medical station, where she found almost unbelievable suffering. Another nun, who arrived in India a year before her, later remembered Teresa as a "great girl, very jolly and bright, full of fun… She didn't know much English in those days, but it was marvelous how she picked it up. She was always a great worker too. Very hard-working. She was also a very kind and **charitable** sort of person, even as a young nun." Sister Teresa took being a nun very seriously—sometimes the other nuns teased her for praying so hard and so often.

"City of Dreadful Night"

In 1931, Teresa took her first **vows** of poverty, **chastity,** and obedience. During this ceremony, she had to lie for some time face down on the floor, as if she were dead. It was meant to show that she was leaving behind all worldly desires. Soon afterward, she left Darjeeling behind too, to begin her teaching career in Calcutta—a place which the English writer Rudyard Kipling, creator of *The Jungle Book,* had once called the "City of Dreadful Night."

In and out of the convent

Although she lived in a slum area of Calcutta, for many years Teresa saw little of the suffering on the streets around her. High walls separated her **convent** and the land around it from the rest of the city. Teresa taught in English at Loreto Entally, a boarding school for girls from broken homes, orphans, and children with only one parent. She also taught geography, then history, in the Bengali language at St. Mary's school nearby. She was a lively and popular teacher, and soon after she took her final lifetime vows in 1937, she became principal of St. Mary's.

> "Dear child, do not forget that you went to India for the sake of the poor."
> A reminder for Teresa in a letter from her mother

There was then a huge upheaval, as World War Two (1939–45) raged and India took its often violent path to **independence.** Teresa began to wonder if God was calling her to work for him beyond the safety of the convent walls.

"A festering labyrinth…"

The writer Rumer Godden lived in Calcutta from the mid-1920s until 1939. In describing the huge city's poorer areas, she later recalled:

"a festering **labyrinth** of little narrow streets… people living on pavements, whole **Eurasian** families in two rooms with very little furniture, and a naked light bulb. The meat safe was usually on a shady wall to keep all the food in. It was very **squalid.** The streets were crowded with **lepers,** begging all amongst the people, **smallpox** was rampant and you did see babies in dustbins. What was horrifying then was that no one did anything about it."
Rumer Godden, in conversation with Anne Sebba, 1995

"A CALL WITHIN A CALL"

T eresa heard this "call within a call," as she described it, on September 10, 1946, when she was 36 years old. (The sisters of the **order** that Teresa later founded now celebrate this date every year as Inspiration Day.) She discussed her new plan with a **Jesuit** priest, Father Celeste Van Exem. He could see how badly she wished to leave the teaching order, to care for the people of the slums, and maybe to start an order of her own for that purpose. "She was not an exceptional person," he recalled. "She was an ordinary Loreto nun, a very ordinary person, but with a great love for her Lord."

A PERIOD OF PROBATION

It was no small matter for a nun to be released from the **convent** to work on the streets of Calcutta.

Indians celebrate the end of their long struggle for independence from Great Britain. Mother Teresa was just beginning her struggle against poverty.

The message was clear

"This is how it happened," Teresa told her spiritual director, Father Julien Henry. "I was travelling to Darjeeling by train, when I heard the voice of God." Father Henry then asked her how she had heard His voice above the noise of a rattling train and she had replied, with a smile, "I was sure it was God's voice. I was certain that He was calling me. The message was clear. I must leave the convent to help the poor by living among them. This was a command, something to be done, something definite. I knew where I had to be. But I did not know how to get there."

From *Mother Teresa: Beyond the Image* by Anne Sebba, 1997

Teresa had to wait until July 1948 to hear that the church **authorities** had granted her wish—but only for one year. She still had to keep her nun's **vows** of poverty, **chastity,** and obedience, but now she had twelve months to prove that she could do useful work in the city.

She spent some time learning basic nursing skills with the Medical Mission Sisters in nearby Patna. She found out how to give shots, deliver a baby, and make beds with hospital corners. Here, too, she changed from her **habit** into a cheap white cotton **sari**, which was far more practical in the heat. This would become Teresa's uniform for her new life— a life that began when she returned to Calcutta, alone, but full of determination to succeed, in December 1948.

"THE POOREST OF THE POOR"

Now that Teresa was free to work in the **bustees,** or slums, of Calcutta, what was she to do? At first she did what she knew best—teaching. In the area called Moti Jhil, she gathered a group of eager children around her and taught them by writing in the mud with a big stick. Teresa was never very good at making plans for the future, but she wasn't worried. She firmly believed that, as long as she was obeying God's call, he would always direct her.

A NEW HOME

For some time, Teresa kept so busy that she got little sleep. She often wandered the streets at night, giving help to whoever needed it. "Oh God!" she wrote in her diary, "If I cannot help these people in their poverty and their suffering, let me at least die with them, close to them so that in that way I can show them your love." Things improved in February 1949, when she moved into a room in a large house at 14 Creek Lane. Its owner, a Roman Catholic Indian named Michael Gomes, did not ask her for rent, or for money for the food he provided. Teresa's first full-time helper, a widow named Charu Ma, soon joined her there. More and more children came to be taught, so she rented a hut for the lessons.

Many of the older priests thought Teresa was foolish to be living among the poor. Several young women, however, were inspired by her example. They came to help her, sometimes leaving school before their final exams to do so. Teresa showed in that first year that her work could be worthwhile. At the end of 1949, she became an Indian citizen, then applied to Pope Pius XII in Rome for permission to start her own **order** to continue the job she had begun.

"Our object is to quench the thirst of Jesus Christ on the cross by dedicating ourselves freely to serve the poorest of the poor, according to the work and teaching of our Lord… Our special task will be to proclaim Jesus Christ to all peoples, above all to those who are in our care. We call ourselves **Missionaries** of Charity."

From the constitution of Teresa's new order

MISSIONARIES OF CHARITY

On October 7, 1950, the Pope gave Teresa permission to set up her new **order.** Like other nuns, the **Missionaries** of Charity took **vows** of poverty, **chastity,** and obedience, but they also vowed "to give wholehearted and free service to the poorest of the poor." According to Teresa, "to be able to love the poor and know the poor we must be poor ourselves." So, like her, the sisters were allowed very few possessions. They dressed in simple white cotton **saris** bordered in blue (the color of the Virgin Mary), with a cross pinned to the left

From the start, the Missionaries of Charity had strictly organized days.

- 4:40 Wake up
- 5:00 Prayers, followed by **Mass** and sermon, followed by breakfast and cleaning
- 8:00 Work among poor and needy
- 12:30 Lunch, followed by short rest
- 2:30 Reading and meditation
- 3:00 Tea
- 3:15 Prayers
- 4:30 Afternoon service to the poor, followed by supper
- 9:00 Evening prayers
- 9:45 Bed

Mother Teresa works and prays along with her Missionaries of Charity.

shoulder. As head of this new order, Sister Teresa now became Mother Teresa.

Her **idealism** appealed to many young Indian women who wanted to make their world a better place. Soon, 14 Creek Lane was too small to hold all the new members, and a new headquarters, or Motherhouse, was set up at 54a Lower Circular Road. It was bought very cheaply, with money authorized by the archbishop. More and more free schools were started, too. Slowly but surely, the Missionaries of Charity were making their presence felt. And the more people heard about them, the more **donations** they gave to help the order's work.

A HOME FOR THE DYING

Indian Hindus see death in a different way from Christians. They link it with impurity and pollution, and only people known as **untouchables** are allowed to handle corpses. Often, when the poor were at the point of death, they could be thrown out of their homes to die—thus saving the house from being "tainted." Mother Teresa was upset to see so many people ending their lives on the streets. Her sisters cared for them as best they could, but she begged the Calcutta Corporation to find a place where the poor could "die with dignity and love."

NIRMAL HRIDAY

In August 1952, Mother Teresa got what she wanted: a home for the dying—which she called Nirmal

Hriday (Place of the Pure Heart)—at the sacred Hindu site of Kalighat. "There were a lot of **destitutes,**" recalled an Indian medical service officer in 1979, "and Mother Teresa and her band of helpers would go into the streets and pick them up to die with dignity. She did a lot of good work for people, but more important and significantly, she set an example to the local Hindu population, who were normally only interested in their own family members."

Sometimes, however, Mother Teresa disagreed with her medical helpers at Nirmal Hriday. Many of the sick could not be saved, but others were suffering from diseases that could actually be treated, such as **malnutrition.** Mother Teresa did not always see the difference. A visitor once saw the sisters ask her to save a boy of sixteen who was on the verge of death, but she simply blessed him and said, "Never mind, it's a lovely day to go to Heaven."

A ruthless woman?

Dr. Marcus Fernandes worked as a volunteer at Nirmal Hriday. His wife, Patricia, later worked on several of Mother Teresa's projects. In 1994, she recalled, "I met Mother Teresa on many occasions… My assessment… was that she was an extremely ruthless and hard woman… My husband had quite severe differences of opinion with her and she would never listen or take any advice on anything… She could only cope with uneducated people, the sort she could shout orders at."

BRANCHING OUT

In 1955, Mother Teresa started a children's home, called Shishu Bhavan, in a rented building just a block away from the Motherhouse. By 1958, there was room for 90 homeless, abandoned, sick, or poor children. At first, she accepted a government **grant** to help pay for this, but the government insisted that she spend exactly 33 **rupees** on each child. Soon she stopped taking this money, since she wanted to take in more children and spend only 17 rupees on each one. As a result, some of her critics said she was "spreading herself too thinly"—trying to do too

Sisters care for the dying in one of the wards at Nirmal Hriday.

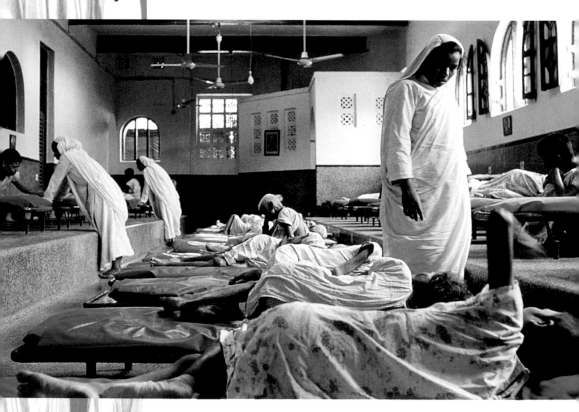

much for too many, and thus not
making a big difference to those
she did help. "But there are so
many needing help," was her reply.
Often, the children were tiny
babies, left to die by families who
could not support them.

> "What I admired most
> in Mother Teresa was
> that she never gave
> the feeling of being
> harassed or stressed;
> that was a big
> motivation. In the
> days before she
> traveled, she always
> had time for
> everyone."
> Lady Aruna Paul,
> 1995

TAKING TREATMENT TO THE SUFFERING

Early in 1956, with $5,000 from
Catholic Relief Services in New
York, the **Missionaries** set up
their first mobile clinic. This
converted van went into some of the city's poorest
areas, providing free medical services. Then, in the
next year, another mobile clinic was set up—this
time for Calcutta's 30,000 **lepers.** Each week, it
carried medicines and equipment to four centers in
the **bustee** areas of Howrah, Tiljala, Dhappa, and
Moti Jhil. A year later, the number of stations visited
had risen to eight. But by the late 1950s, Mother
Teresa was beginning to look beyond Calcutta, even
beyond India.

Mother Teresa masterminded the **order's** expansion
with great energy, but she remained as calm as ever,
despite all the demands made on her.

OVERSEAS EXPANSION

According to Roman Catholic law, new **orders** must wait for ten years before opening other houses. Mother Teresa's order was ten years old in 1960, when she herself was fifty. By that time she had 119 sisters, mostly Indian, following her **rule,** but she was eager to spread her message further. So she sent groups of sisters to begin similar work in the states of Bihar and Uttar Pradesh, and in India's capital city, New Delhi. In the following years, more homes and services were set up all over India. After introducing a mobile clinic leprosy service at Asansol, West Bengal, the order founded a town for **lepers,** called Shanti Nagar.

"POOR ON THE MOON"

By 1960, people around the world were beginning to hear about Mother Teresa and her work. Her fame increased after she went **abroad** to address the National Council for Catholic Women in Las Vegas, Nevada. From there, she traveled widely in the United States and Europe before returning to India. She was not a gifted public speaker—and she never spoke English fluently—but she impressed many people by her simple sincerity. And although she never begged for money for her work, saying instead that she depended upon God to provide, people still contributed very generously.

On her travels, she saw that there were poor people needing help even in supposedly **affluent** countries. In 1965, Pope Paul VI gave her permission to set up homes in these countries, too. The first, in Cocorote, Venezuela, was opened in July of 1965. In 1968, one was opened in the slums of Rome, and in 1969, a center for **aborigines** was started at Bourke, Australia. Throughout the 1970s, every six months or so, a new **Missionaries** of Charity center would open somewhere in the world. "If there are poor on the moon, we shall go there too," Mother Teresa promised.

Patients in Calcutta line up to see a doctor at a clinic.

"SOMETHING BEAUTIFUL FOR GOD"

By the late 1960s, Mother Teresa was quite well known all over the world, especially among Roman Catholics. Then two different British television **documentaries** introduced her to millions more people. The first was *Meeting Point* (1968), when she was interviewed by journalist Malcolm Muggeridge in London. Small and wrinkled, the old nun spoke simply but movingly about her work. She made no appeal for money, but viewers sent in almost $50,000 anyway.

WITNESSING A MIRACLE?

The second TV program, made by Muggeridge and a British crew in Calcutta, had an even greater impact. At first, Mother Teresa did not want to be

In the 1960s, many people began to look to India and Indian ways for spiritual guidance. The Beatles and their friends were some of them.

filmed "in action," but finally she agreed, "if this TV program is going to help people love better." It took five days to make the 50-minute documentary. When Muggeridge returned to England, Mother Teresa wrote to him, "I can't tell you how big a sacrifice it was to accept the making of a film—but I am glad now that I did so because it has brought us all closer to God. In your own way try to make the world conscious that it is never too late to do something beautiful for God."

Those last four words became the title of the moving black-and-white film that was first shown in 1969. Millions of viewers were now astonished to see for themselves what the **Missionaries** of Charity were doing among Calcutta's poor. TV cameras even filmed inside Nirmal Hriday, and although it was rather dark in there, the resulting pictures seemed to be bathed in a golden light. To some, this was nothing short of a miracle, making Mother Teresa herself seem almost saintly.

INTERNATIONAL RECOGNITION

By 1970, there were 585 sisters in Mother Teresa's order, of whom 332 had **professed** their final **vows.** Year by year, new recruits—from Venezuela, Malaysia, Nepal, Italy, and many other countries—were joining at an even greater rate than before. In addition, an increasing number of **lay** assistants belonged to the **order's** International Association of Co-Workers.

Among other projects, the Co-Workers encouraged children from the world's wealthier nations to help the starving poor of India. As a result of the "bread campaign" in the United Kingdom (U.K.), British boys and girls saved enough pennies to give a daily slice of bread to 5,000 poor Indian schoolchildren. Thousands of Danish children "made beautiful sacrifices" to provide a daily glass of milk.

Mother Teresa, as the head of such a successful international organization, won the admiration of many people. Among her supporters were presidents and other leading politicians whom she met on her travels. She was never shy around "important" people, and if she felt that they could help with one of her projects, she did not hesitate to let them know. She asked Indian Prime Minister Indira Gandhi if she could be a flight attendant on Indian Airlines, so she

could keep in touch with all her **Missionary** homes without spending money on airfare. Mrs. Gandhi responded in 1973 by giving her a free air pass.

A RELUCTANT HEROINE

Mother Teresa received a stream of awards and prizes in recognition of her work, ranging from the Pope John XXIII Peace Prize in 1971 to the American "Master et Magistra" Award in 1974. In 1975, the United Nations made its Ceres Medal in her honor. She was also given a number of titles from universities and colleges, including an honorary doctorate of divinity from Cambridge University in the U.K. She accepted the praise with humility and good humor. "I never know whether I should accept or not," she once said, "it means nothing to me. But it gives me a chance to speak of Christ to people who otherwise may not hear of him." She knew, too, that when she spoke in public, she usually managed to convert more listeners to join her worldwide **crusade**—and the poor could always use any prize money she won.

Mother Teresa
received the
Nobel Peace Prize
at a ceremony in
Oslo in 1979.

NOBEL PRIZE WINNER

Throughout the 1970s, Malcolm Muggeridge and others launched a campaign for Mother Teresa to be given the Nobel Peace Prize. In 1972, when the judges in Oslo, Norway, asked Muggeridge what she had done for world peace, he replied, "By dedicating her life wholly to Christ, by seeing in every suffering soul her Savior and treating them accordingly,… she was…along with her **Missionaries** of Charity, a sort of powerhouse of love in the world."

But in that year, in 1975, and again in 1977, the **lucrative** and **prestigious** prize went to someone else. "I had a good laugh," Mother Teresa remarked after the third disappointment. "It will come only when Jesus thinks it is time. We have all calculated to build two hundred homes for the **lepers** if it comes, so our people will have to do the praying." Then at last, in 1979, she won.

"MOTHER OF THE WORLD"

In December 1979, Mother Teresa went to Oslo to receive her medal and a check for $190,000—as well as a further $70,000 raised by young people in

Norway. Usually, there would have been a celebration banquet, costing $6,000, but she asked the organizers to cancel it and spend the money on the poor instead. As a Nobel Prize winner, her fame soared to even greater heights. "You have been the Mother of Bengal," Jyoti Basu, an Indian politician, told her at a special reception. "Now you are the Mother of the World."

Mother Teresa took every public opportunity to spread the word about her work.

"The year 1979 has not been a year of peace. Disputes and conflicts between nations, peoples, and **ideologies** have been conducted with all the accompanying extremes of inhumanity and cruelty. We have witnessed wars, the unrestrained use of violence,... fanaticism hand in hand with cynicism... contempt for human life and dignity... The Norwegian Nobel Committee has considered it right and appropriate, precisely in this year, in their choice of Mother Teresa to remind the world of the words spoken by Fridtjof Nansen: 'Love of one's neighbor is realistic policy.'"

From the address of Professor John Sannes, chairman of the Norwegian Nobel Committee, in Oslo, 1979

TOO MANY CHILDREN?

M other Teresa always spoke from the heart, but despite her obvious sincerity, her views sometimes surprised people and even seemed insensitive. On receiving her Nobel Prize in Oslo, she made headlines with a speech condemning abortion. She called it "the greatest destroyer of peace today… because it is a direct war, a direct killing, direct murder by the mother herself." Her sisters, she said, had saved thousands of lives by telling Indian clinics, hospitals, and police stations, "Please don't destroy the child; we will take the child… And also we are doing another thing which is very beautiful. We are teaching our beggars, our leprosy patients, our slum dwellers, our people of the street, natural family planning." This meant using the **rhythm method,** the only kind of birth control approved by the Roman Catholic Church.

"Human life must be respected and protected absolutely from the moment of conception… Since it must be treated from conception as a person, the **embryo** must be defended in its integrity, cared for, and healed as far as possible like any other human being."
From 1992 Catholic Church Catechism

MURDER OR MERCY KILLING?

In a heavily overpopulated world, not everyone agreed with views like these. Mother Teresa was called unrealistic for holding them. Feminists claimed that it was a woman's right to decide whether or not to have children. But she would

not **compromise.** At a prayer breakfast with President Clinton in 1995, she flatly stated, "As I am the pencil of God, I know what God likes and does not like. He does not like abortion and **contraception.**" Someone present later said, "Many in the audience clearly felt that this was arrogance to the point of rudeness, but there were also some, I know, who felt a deep appreciation of what she was saying."

"Mother Teresa told Malcolm Muggeridge that there could never be too many children in India because God always provides. 'He provides for the flowers and the birds and for everything in the world that he has created. And those little children are his life. There can never be enough.' Charming though that is, it somehow misses the point. Of course, once children exist everything must be done to look after them. But, sadly, there is not always the provision for them... Ten years after this comment Mother Teresa admitted to a *Newsweek* reporter that overpopulation was a serious problem."

From *Mother Teresa: Beyond the Image* by Anne Sebba, 1997

GOD'S GLOBETROTTER

Mother Teresa and Diana, Princess of Wales, respected and admired one another. In their different ways, they successfully raised funds to support charities around the world.

In the years after Mother Teresa won the Nobel Peace Prize, political and business leaders were more eager than ever to speak with her and be photographed with her at 54a Lower Circular Road, and then give more money to the **Missionaries** of Charity. She also received many more invitations from **abroad** to make speeches or to visit refugee camps in the world's trouble spots—where she did much more than simply talk.

BACK HOME

In 1980, she even had the chance to return to Skopje, the town where she was born. So much had

> "What stunned everyone was her energy and efficiency. She saw the problem, fell to her knees and prayed for a few seconds and then she was rattling off a list of supplies she needed—nappies [diapers], plastic pants, chamber pots. The problem is that in wartime most of the attention is focused on the casualties. But the blind, the deaf, the insane, and the spastics tend to be forgotten just when they need help the most. Mother Teresa understood that right away."
>
> An International Red Cross official in Beirut in war-torn Lebanon, 1982

happened since her departure at the age of eighteen. Her brother, Lazar, had left the **Balkans** too. In 1960, Mother Teresa had arranged to meet him when she was in Italy, but she was never able to see her sister, Age, and her mother again. For decades, they had lived in Albania, which had become a Communist country. Now its borders were closed to most of the rest of the world.

During the 1980s, Mother Teresa was sometimes away from India for ten months of each year, but her **order's** work showed no sign of slowing. In 1979, there were 158 Missionaries of Charity houses in the world. In the next year, fourteen more were opened, then eighteen in the next. By 1982, there were 81 homes for the poor and dying, which served 13,000 people, and six million sick people were being treated by 670 mobile clinics.

SAINT AMONG THE SINNERS?

In the mid–1980s, Mother Teresa caused a stir in New York by arranging for three violent prisoners to be transferred from Sing Sing Prison into the sisters' care at a special hospital. This was because the prisoners had the fatal disease AIDS.

"We plan to give them tender loving care because each one is Jesus in a distressing disguise," she said. "We are not here to sit in judgement on these people, to decide blame or guilt. Our mission is to help them to make their dying days more tolerable and we have sisters who are dedicated to do that." But according to the doctor at the hospital, the sisters had no idea what AIDS was or how to deal with the disease. "The crucifix on your chest isn't going to protect you," the doctor warned them. "God will provide," Mother Teresa replied.

Mother Teresa visits a sick child in Bhopal, India.

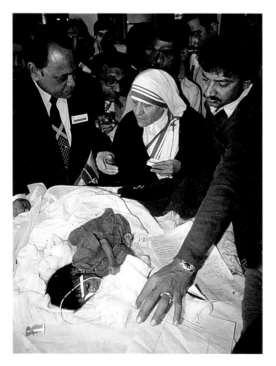

ETHIOPIAN MERCY MISSION

In 1985, Mother Teresa visited Ethiopia at the height of its terrible **famine.** Her **order** was already at work in the capital, Addis Ababa, and ran a feeding program and hospital in the

Rock star Bob Geldof offered to perform a benefit concert in India for the order. Mother Teresa said there was no need—God would provide.

province of Wollo; now she wanted to see what more she could do. The **media** were fascinated by her meeting with foul-mouthed, hard-living rock star Bob Geldof, who had raised huge amounts of money for Ethiopia with his **Band Aid** project. "What you do I could not do," she told him, "and what I do you could not do. But as long as it is clear in your heart and your mind, then it is God's will to see us through."

"She was astonishingly tiny. When I went to greet her I found that I towered more than two feet above her. She was a battered, wizened woman. The thing that struck me most forcefully was her feet. Her **habit** was clean and well cared for but her sandals were beaten-up pieces of leather from which her feet protruded, gnarled and misshapen as old tree roots... [then when he bent to kiss her] she bowed her head so swiftly that I was obliged to kiss the top of her **wimple.** It disturbed me. I found out later that she only let **lepers** kiss her."

From *Is That It?*, the **autobiography** of Bob Geldof, 1986

A POLITICAL ANIMAL?

In his 1994 book *An Intimate History of Humanity,* Theodore Zeldin of Oxford University wrote that, in the modern world, "Power no longer ensures respect. Even the most powerful person in the world, the President of the United States, is not powerful enough to command everybody's respect; he probably has less than Mother Teresa, whom nobody is obliged to obey." Many politicians must have envied Mother Teresa for the global respect she enjoyed. But she herself was careful to treat politicians well. This was partly because she knew they had the power and **resources** to help her in her work. By being respectful, she could also hope to influence their other actions.

"Dear President George Bush and President Saddam Hussein, I come to you with tears in my eyes and God's love in my heart to plead to you for the poor and those who will become poor if the war that we all dread and fear happens. I beg you with my whole heart to work for, to labour for God's peace and to be reconciled with one another... In the short term there may be winners and losers in this war that we all dread, but that never can, nor ever will justify the suffering, pain and loss of life which your weapons will cause."

From a letter to the U.S. and Iraqi presidents
on the eve of the Gulf War, 1991

Mother Teresa meets Yasir Arafat, chairman of the Palestinian Liberation Organization, who was regarded by many as a brutal terrorist.

ABOVE POLITICS?

Sometimes Mother Teresa's willingness to greet and be greeted by political leaders caused concern. In 1980, she visited Haiti, one of the world's poorest countries, yet she had nothing but praise for rich and **despotic** President Duvalier and his wife. Then, in 1989, she was finally allowed to enter Albania, where she laid a bouquet on the tombstone of Enver Hoxha, the country's brutal Communist ruler who had died four years before. According to Dr. Jack Preger, who once worked for her in Calcutta, "Mother Teresa is prepared to shake hands with any type of murderer who happens to be in political power." But she usually had her reasons. After meeting with the Albanian **authorities,** for example, she was allowed to set up two houses where her sisters could start work in that desperately needy country.

PROBLEMS IN THE NINETIES

As Mother Teresa entered her eighth decade, her own health became an important issue. Since founding her **order**, she had pushed herself extraordinarily hard. Although she had often been sick as a child, it was almost as if she did not allow herself to become ill during the second, highly active part of her life. But in September 1989, she suffered a serious heart attack and had to undergo major surgery. Two years later, she was treated for heart disease and bacterial pneumonia. Despite her health problems, she kept on traveling, and in 1993, in Rome, she fell and broke her ribs. Within months, she became seriously ill with malaria, complicated by heart and lung problems.

In her later years, Mother Teresa's health was clearly deteriorating.

WHO COULD TAKE HER PLACE?

As early as 1990, she told the Pope that she thought she should resign. However, many people believed her to be irreplaceable as the head of the **Missionaries** of Charity. She was so well-known that she gave the order a wonderfully clear identity, and her matchless reputation encouraged people all over the world to contribute funds.

Mother Teresa herself had never prepared anyone to take her place. "Wait until I die and then see," she would say. Some said that she had always found it hard to **delegate** responsibility. She alone decided, for example, whether a door thousands of miles away should be painted blue or white.

Although she was ill, she continued to lead her order until 1997. Then, on March 13, after weeks of discussions, the Missionaries of Charity announced that a solution had been found. Mother Teresa would stay on as head in name, but another nun would take on the day-to-day chores of running the order. The new Superior General was to be Sister Nirmala, a shy 63-year-old woman who had converted from Hinduism to Christianity.

As events turned out, this arrangement lasted for less than a year, for on September 5, 1997—the day of Princess Diana's funeral—Mother Teresa died of a heart attack at the Motherhouse.

Sister Nirmala has had the difficult task of succeeding Mother Teresa as head of the Missionaries of Charity.

GOING HOME TO GOD

At the time of Mother Teresa's death, her **order** had more than 4,000 sisters and nearly 600 homes in well over 100 different countries. But the great sense of loss was felt by many millions more around the world. Her **embalmed** body was placed under a glass dome in St. Thomas's Church, Calcutta, and in the next week, huge crowds filed past to pay their last respects. Meanwhile, it was announced that Mother Teresa would be given the honor of a state funeral, which would be arranged by the army. To some, this seemed a peculiar outcome for a woman who had worked so tirelessly all her life for peace.

On Saturday, September 13, her body was transported to the 12,000-seat Netaji indoor stadium, where 400 international dignitaries were among the mourners. The four-mile route was lined by 100,000 people. Then millions watched the two-and-a-half-hour funeral service on TV. Representatives of the six major faiths in India—Christian, Hindu, Muslim, Sikh, Buddhist, and Parsee—spoke in praise of Mother Teresa. Finally, with rain pouring down, her coffin was taken to the Motherhouse for private burial there. A 21-gun salute announced that the body had been lowered into the ground; then four soldiers sounded bugles. On her grave was carved, "Love one another as I have loved you."

WAS SHE A SAINT?

Before she died, Mother Teresa spoke without fear of "going home to God." She fully expected St. Peter to recognize her as she approached Heaven's gates, "and he will say, 'but what have you done, Mother Teresa, filling up paradise with all your poor people?'" She herself was believed by many to be a saint during her lifetime. However, saints have to be canonized, or officially declared, by the highest officials of the Roman

The coffin of Mother Teresa was carried through the streets at her funeral in September 1997.

Catholic Church, and becoming a saint is a very long, slow process. Church officials must investigate the person's life and works, and learn about any miracles that they are supposed to have performed. Usually, this process does not even begin until the person has been dead for five years. However, Cardinal Joseph Ratzinger, a close adviser to Pope John Paul II, has hinted that in Mother Teresa's case this process could be "less long." Few people will be surprised if the "Saint of the Slums" is made an official saint very soon.

'The Teresa cult is now a **missionary** multi-national, with annual turnover in the tens of millions. If concentrated in Calcutta, that could certainly support a large hospital, perhaps even make a noticeable difference. But Mother Teresa has chosen instead to spread her franchise very thinly. To her, the **convent** and the catechism matter more than the clinic."

From *Hell's Angel*, a British TV **documentary** made by Christopher Hitchens, 1994

"DON'T LOOK FOR NUMBERS"

Few people publicly criticized Mother Teresa or her work until the last few years of her life. For decades, she was seen as an almost holy figure herself, especially in Europe and the U.S. It hardly seemed right to find fault, since she was so clearly a selfless, decent woman who was doing a great deal of good.

But as the writer Anne Sebba pointed out towards the end of Mother Teresa's life, "after fifty years, the world of charity has moved on. Those who give are, by and large, no longer prepared to do so in the vague hope that it does some good somewhere." Some critics now believe that instead of helping individual people who were poor or sick, the Missionaries of Charity should have tried to attack poverty and disease at the roots, by treating the causes, not the symptoms.

Mother Teresa disagreed. When she heard her efforts described as small drops in an ocean of need, she would reply, "I do not add up. I only subtract from the total number of poor or dying." One of her biographers, Kathryn Spink, wrote, "The call to change social structures and deal with the root cause of collective problems was a valid one, but it was for others. 'Begin in a small way,' she directed those who worked with her. 'Don't look for numbers.'"

The Gospel of love

Pope John Paul II, a close friend and supporter of Mother Teresa, was too ill to attend her funeral, so he sent the Vatican secretary of state, Cardinal Angelo Sodano, in his place. In his tribute, Sodano said that Mother Teresa had been fully aware of criticisms of her. "It has been said that Mother Teresa might have done more to fight the causes of poverty in the world. She would shrug as if saying, 'while you go on discussing causes and explanations, I will kneel beside the poorest of the poor and attend to their needs. The dying, the handicapped and defenseless unborn… need a loving presence and a caring hand.' Mother Teresa of Calcutta understood fully the Gospel of love."

A young boy, with a photo of Mother Teresa, watches her funeral procession in September 1997.

MOTHER TERESA— TIMELINE

1910 Agnes Gonxha Bojaxhiu born in Skopje (August 26)

1928 (September) Agnes leaves to join the Sisters of Loreto in Ireland; becomes Sister Teresa (December) Sails for India

1929 Sister Teresa starts teaching in Darjeeling

1931 Sister Teresa takes her first **vows** of poverty, **chastity,** and obedience, and is sent to Calcutta to teach

1937 Sister Teresa takes her final vows and become principal of St. Mary's school

1946 Sister Teresa hears the "call within a call" and asks to leave the **convent** to help the poor by living among them

1948 Sister Teresa, wearing a white **sari,** leaves the convent to begin her new work

1949 Sister Teresa becomes an Indian citizen

1950 Pope Pius XII approves the founding of Mother Teresa's **Missionaries** of Charity **Order**

1952 Nirmal Hriday, home for the dying, set up

1953 Missionaries move into their Motherhouse in Calcutta

1955 Shishu Bhavan, the first children's home, opens

1960 Mother Teresa begins a period of extensive foreign travel

1965 Missionaries' first overseas house opens, in Venezuela

1969 *Something Beautiful for God* shown on British television

1975 United Nations Ceres medal made in Mother Teresa's honor

1979 Mother Teresa wins the Nobel Peace Prize

1990 Sick Mother Teresa suggests to the Pope that she should resign, but does not

1997 (March) Mother Teresa finally gives up day-to-day running of the order

(September 5) Mother Teresa dies—and the campaign begins to make her a saint

Kindly thank the people of the whole world and the woodland people for all their prayer and tender love and care I have received God bless you M Teresa mc

Mother Teresa wrote this message of thanks in 1989, during her recovery after heart problems while staying at the Woodlands Nursing Home in Calcutta.

GLOSSARY

aborigine person of the race that first lived in Australia

abroad in another country

affluent rich

aristocratic noble or high-born

authority person who holds power

autobiography book written by a person about his own life

Balkans southeastern region of Europe

Band Aid money-raising project featuring pop musicians, led by Bob Geldof

baptize to receive a person officially into the Christian church and give him or her a name

bustee Indian slum district

charitable generous

chastity agreement not to have sexual relations, marry, or have children

chronic continuing for a long time or returning often

communion bread and wine received in a church service

compromise agreement where two sides each give in a little

contraception deliberately preventing pregnancy

convent group of nuns living together, or the building in which they live

crusade vigorous campaign to achieve something worthwhile

delegate to hand responsibility to someone else in an organization

despotic harsh in ruling

devout deeply religious

destitute very poor person

documentary program about a real-life person or thing

donation gift (usually of money)

embalmed preserved from decay

embryo earliest formation of a baby inside its mother

equerry officer in a royal household

Eurasian person with one European and one Asian parent

famine large-scale shortage of food

grant legal handing over of something, often money

habit dress worn by members of a religious order

hospitality kindness to guests or strangers

humanitarian person who tries to improve human welfare

idealism aiming high in one's thinking and planning

ideology set of ideas about how people should lead their lives

independent (country) ruling over itself, not part of another country

Jesuit member of a Roman Catholic religious order founded in 1534 by Ignatius Loyola

labyrinth maze

lay (brother or sister) not a full member of a religious order

leper person with leprosy, a serious and contagious disease that affects the skin and the nervous system

lucrative money-making

malnutrition condition of not getting enough to eat, or not eating the right foods

Mass Catholic church service

media plural of medium (of communication), e.g. newspapers, TV, or radio

missionary religious person who goes to help and teach the poor

novice (nun) trainee sister

order (religious) group of men or women who bind themselves with vows to devote themselves to religious aims

pastor minister in charge of a church or congregation

pilgrimage journey to a sacred place as an act of religious devotion

prestigious well worth having, of very high reputation, valuable

professed (nuns) nuns who have taken the vows of their religious order

Protestant Reformation revolutionary event in Europe in the sixteenth century which led to the setting up of first "Protestant" churches alongside Catholic ones

redemption being saved or forgiven for sins

resources (financial) funds

rhythm method system of birth control based on avoiding sexual intercourse at times of the month when the woman is producing eggs

rule code of discipline observed by a religious order

rupee money unit of India and Pakistan

sari traditional dress of Hindu women, made of a single piece of cloth

shrine place that is considered holy, usually because of something that happened there or someone who is buried there

smallpox contagious viral disease

sodality Roman Catholic religious society

squalid filthy, usually because of poverty

untouchable Hindu who is born into a group low down on the social ladder

vow solemn and serious promise

wimple nun's headdress

MORE BOOKS TO READ

Holland, Margaret. *Mother Teresa.* Dublin, Ohio: PAGES Publishing Co., 1992.

Jensen, Anne F. *India: Its Culture and People.* White Plains, N.Y.: Longman Publishing Group, 1991.

Lazo, Caroline. *Mother Teresa.* Columbus, Ohio: Silver Burdett Press, 1993.

Wood, Richard. *Mother Teresa: Saint of the Poor.* Austin, Tex.: Raintree Steck-Vaughn Publishers, 1998.

INDEX